Brave Eagle's Account of

The Fetterman Fight

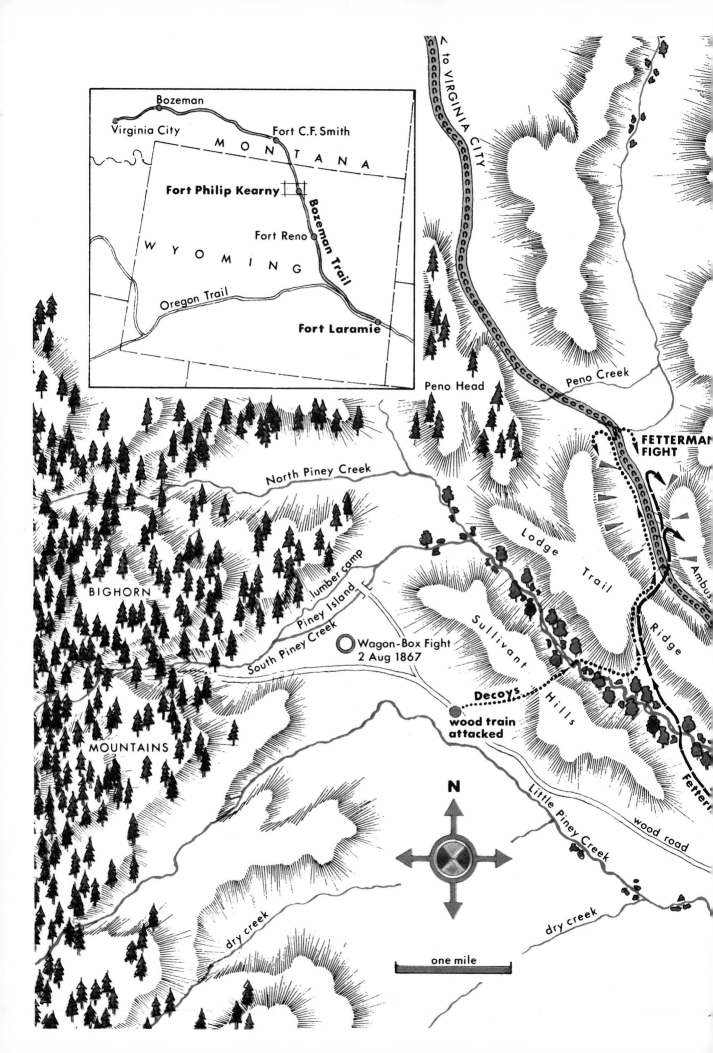

Bozeman

Virginia City

Fort C.F. Smith

M O N T A N A

Fort Philip Kearny

Fort Reno

W Y O M I N G

Bozeman Trail

Oregon Trail

Fort Laramie

to VIRGINIA CITY

Peno Creek

Peno Head

FETTERMAN FIGHT

North Piney Creek

Lodge Trail

lumber camp

Piney Island

BIGHORN

South Piney Creek

Sullivant

Wagon-Box Fight 2 Aug 1867

Ambush Ridge

Hills

Decoys

MOUNTAINS

wood train attacked

Fetterman

N

Little Piney Creek

wood road

dry creek

dry creek

one mile

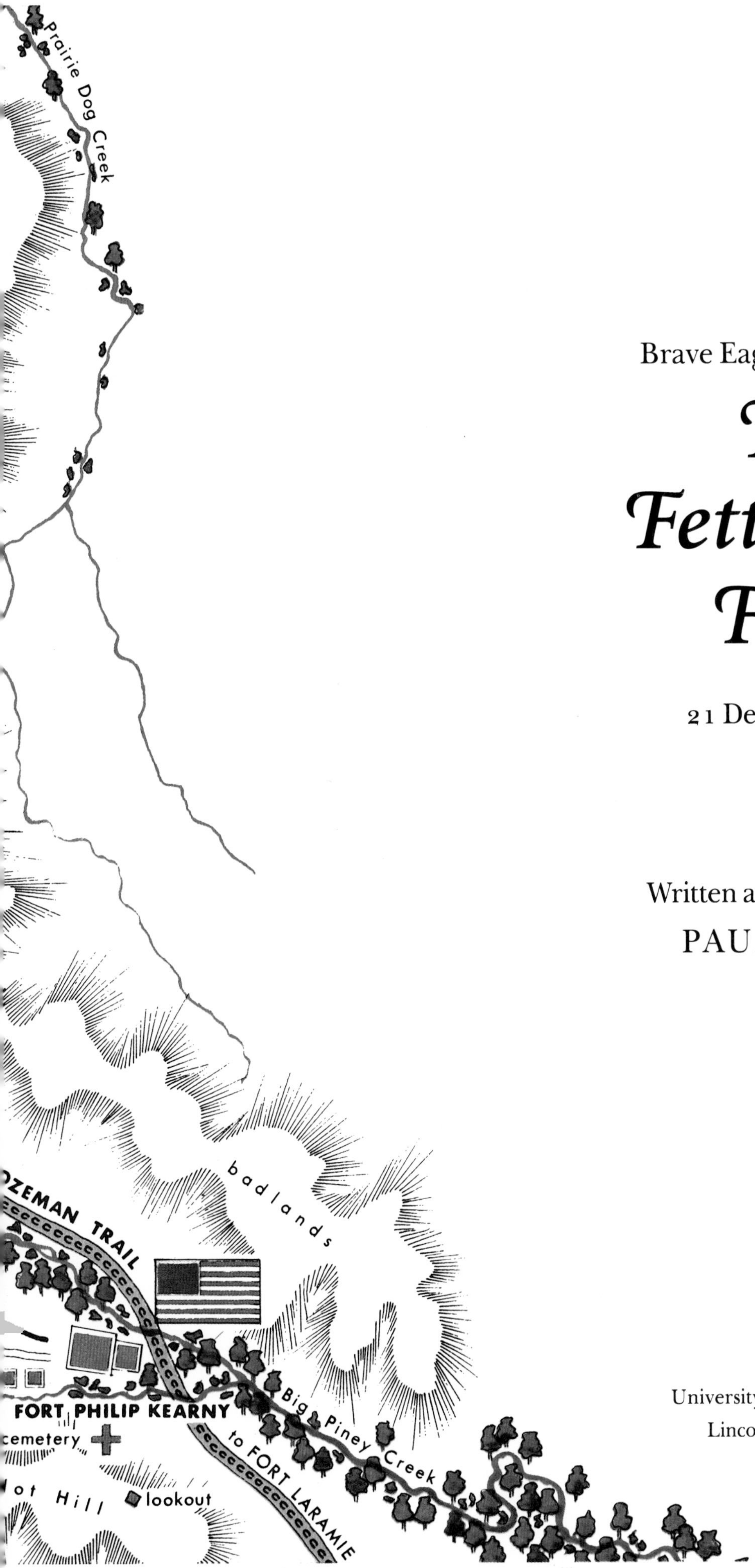

Brave Eagle's Account of

The Fetterman Fight

21 December 1866

Written and illustrated by

PAUL GOBLE

University of Nebraska Press
Lincoln and London

Prairie Dog Creek

badlands

BOZEMAN TRAIL

FORT PHILIP KEARNY

cemetery

ot Hill   lookout

Big Piney Creek

to FORT LARAMIE

Library of Congress
Cataloging-in-Publication Data
Goble, Paul.
Brave Eagle's account of the Fetterman fight,
21 December 1866/
written and illustrated by Paul Goble.
p.   cm. Reprint.
Originally published: New York:
Pantheon Books, 1972.
ISBN 0-8032-7032-1 (pbk.)
1. Fetterman Fight, Wyo., 1866 – Juvenile literature.
2. Red Cloud, 1822–1909 – Juvenile literature.
[1. Fetterman Fight, Wyo., 1866.
2. Red Cloud, 1822–1909.]
I. Title.
II. Title: Fetterman fight.
[E83.866. G62   1992]
973.8'1 – dc20   91-23198
CIP   AC

Brave Eagle's Account of the Fetterman Fight,
by Paul and Dorothy Goble,
was first published in 1972 by Macmillan, London,
and Pantheon Books, New York.
Reprinted by arrangement
with Paul Goble.

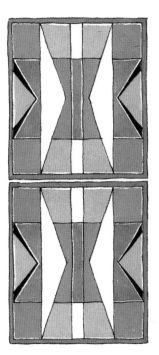

For Edgar Red Cloud, great-grandson of the Chief.

Ate ciyuonihan kin, cajemayakaġe cin on wopila ecicye wacin; canke wowapi cik'ala kin le ci'cu. Wakinyan Cik'ala he miye.

"The white men have surrounded me and have left me nothing but an island. When we first had this land we were strong, now our nation is melting away like snow on the hillsides where the sun is warm; while the white people grow like the blades of grass when summer is coming. I do not want the white people to make any roads through our country."

Red Cloud

AUTHOR'S NOTE TO THE BISON BOOK EDITION

Brave Eagle's Account of The Fetterman Fight was my second book, following three years after *Red Hawk's Account of Custer's Last Battle*. It is easy to look back at one's early work and to be embarrassed by its innocent beginnings, and its mistakes, but one has to start somewhere. In order to make a start it is necessary to be influenced: to be excited and to love something passionately. Readers who know the literature will recognize my influences: the echoes of *Black Elk Speaks* by John G. Neihardt are plain, and the style of ledger-book art in my illustrations is obvious. Twenty-five years later, and having written and illustrated nearly as many books, I still love those books which influenced me so greatly. In time I gradually found my own style of writing, and evolved other ways to draw and paint.

I wrote the book for Indian children because I wanted them to know about and to feel proud of the courage of their ancestors. I have written all my books primarily with Indian children in mind because I firmly believe that what is fine from "buffalo days" can be transferred to life in these "automobile days." The essential truths contained in the mythology never change. They are like an anchor. Similarly the examples of their great leaders of history can be taken for today's inspiration.

The book was written in the early 1970s, at the time when the American Indian Movement was strong. I saw the AIM leaders in the image of the warriors I was writing about. It is fashionable to denigrate the movement, but as far as I was concerned they were courageously defending their people against the ever continuing aggression. It was an exciting period which influenced everyone in some way or another; I am sure a few extra warlike adjectives and bloodthirsty phrases were added to the book as a result.

I remember, and wish to express my gratitude to, Fr. Gall Schuon (named *Lakota Isnala* by Nicholas Black Elk), whose many letters helped me with the story and illustrations. I also remember Marco Pallis, who helped me with the writing.

AUTHOR'S NOTE

What is known of the fight was told in later years by the Indians who had fought in it, and so it seems appropriate that it should be retold by them. This account attempts to capture the spirit of the published Indian accounts, but because Indians told only what they saw and did, it has also been necessary to draw on the material of white historians, in order to give the reader a better understanding of the fight and the events which preceded it. Many of the words spoken by Red Cloud in this account are edited extracts from his recorded speeches.

THE BACKGROUND

In 1866 the process of driving the Indians from their lands and containing them within reservations was nearing its final stages. The Civil War had ended and the nation's resources were directed toward healing the wounds inflicted during the five terrible years of bloodshed and destruction. The nation was tired of war. While reconstruction was going on, the authorities in Washington hoped they could avoid military conflict with the Indian tribes, but at the same time they realized nothing could halt the civilian expansion westward.

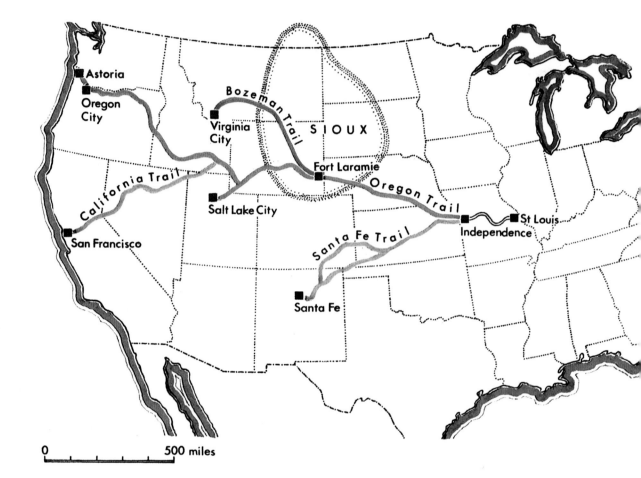

Astoria

Oregon City

Bozeman Trail

Virginia City

SIOUX

California Trail

Fort Laramie

Oregon Trail

Salt Lake City

St Louis

Independence

San Francisco

Santa Fe Trail

Santa Fe

0   500 miles

The powerful Sioux and Cheyenne tribes posed the greatest threat; the administration decided it would be cheaper to appease them, if possible, than to fight them. A commission was sent out to Fort Laramie in June to make peace and to give presents to the Indians; at the same time the commission hoped to secure the Indians' agreement to a right of way through their lands.

The right of way which they wanted was the Bozeman Trail leading to the gold mines of Virginia City farther to the west. It was the shortest route and had been unofficially used for several years, but at great risk of Indian attacks. Red Cloud, war chief of the Oglala Sioux, and many other chiefs were determined to prohibit the use of the trail because it passed through their best hunting grounds, disturbing the buffalo and other game upon which they depended.

Whether the commission would succeed or fail in its attempt to gain the Indians' assent, Washington had already decided to give military protection to civilians who wished to use the trail; and Colonel Henry Carrington, with seven hundred men, was ordered to build forts along the trail, to protect it. The members of the commission were confident that Colonel Carrington would handle any opposition which Red Cloud and the other hostile chiefs might offer. Having obtained the agreement of a few peaceful or uninterested chiefs, they returned to Washington and declared the Bozeman Trail open and safe for travel.

They had grossly underestimated the Indians' determination. At no time, even after the forts had been built, was travel safe, and for long periods the trail was quite impassable. Far from giving protection, the soldiers could do no more than protect themselves inside their own forts. Within six months after the commission left Fort Laramie, the army suffered its worst defeat by the Indians, up to that time, in an engagement known as the Fetterman Fight. Captain Fetterman's entire command of eighty-two men were killed by overwhelming numbers of Sioux and Cheyennes led by Red Cloud.

Brave Eagle's Account of

The Fetterman Fight

21 December 1866

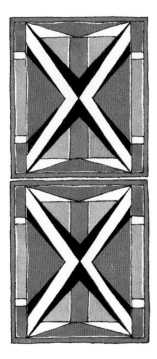

BRAVE EAGLE BEGINS

I was just nineteen years old that spring when Big Ribs and some of our people who were living around Fort Laramie came to our camp on Powder River. They said that white men had come from the Great White Father in Washington and they wanted to smoke the pipe with our chiefs and make peace. "They are important men," Big Ribs said, "dressed in black suits and tall shiny hats. Those who want to be friends, these white men say, should come at once and make their mark on a piece of paper. They will give a great feast for all the people and more presents than you can carry home with you." *Ho!* "Guns and plenty of ammunition as well." *Washtay!* Good!

"Tell the white men," Red Cloud answered Big Ribs, "that the bands of my people are scattered far and that our horses are too weak after the long winter to travel now. But tell them that we shall be at the Soldiers' Town before two moons have passed and that we will come in peace with our women and little children."

There was talking and arguing in the camps for many days about whether we should go to Fort Laramie. Sitting Bull and Crazy Horse said they would not go to talk with the white men, and there were many among us who agreed that nothing good ever came from talking with them. Crazy Horse said, "The white men will tell you that the land they have is not enough and that you must give them more, and they will make you touch the pen. Do not trust the white men; they are never satisfied with what they have. Remember that the Great Spirit gave this land to the Oglalas and one does not sell the earth upon which the people walk."

The chiefs and warriors talked. I hoped we would go because I wanted to taste some of the white man's food which our relatives, the stay-around-the-fort people, spoke so much about.

And we went as Red Cloud had said we would. We traveled slowly, with the bands spread out because there were no enemies to be feared, and we camped where there was good grass for the horses at night. When we were near Fort Laramie the soldiers came out to meet us, marching in long lines with those in front making music. They led us to where the stay-around-the-fort people were camped, and the women set up the tipis next to them.

Everyone was happy. At last peace would be made with the white man. There had been war between us for as long as I could remember.

The women were excited to see great piles of presents being unloaded for us from wagons onto a flat place beyond the camp. The soldiers who were guarding them said there were many fine things for the women, and guns for us as well. It was difficult to wait.

The council started the next day. The Great White Father's men did not look very important; they had not painted their faces and their hair was cut short as if in mourning. I did not go close to them, but some people said they smelled like the spotted buffalo they eat. Many strange things were spoken of them. That was the first time I ever saw white women and I thought they were good to look at, with beautiful skin like the petals of the wild rose. But their bodies looked weak, and a man must have a strong woman who can carry wood and water to his tipi and one who walks with long strides to keep up when moving camp.

The white men talked among themselves as white people always do, talking all together and not really listening to what the others say.

When the pipe had been lit, Red Cloud rose. He raised it in silent prayer to the sky above and touched it to the earth beneath. Then he turned, offering smoke to each of the four quarters of the world: to the west which is the power of the thunder and the life-giving rain; to the north from where the purifying winds come with the snow; to the east with the day-break star and the rising sun; and turning to the south he offered the pipe to the beginning and end of all life. The white men watched; but they did not understand. The pipe was then passed around the circle and when all had smoked, Red Cloud spoke what was in all our hearts:

"My brothers and my friends, the Great Spirit placed me and my people on this land. When the white men first came we gave them some of our land and we did not wish to hurt them. But the white people wanted more and drove us back and took more land. Now you have come from the Great White Father and have offered us peace, and we are happy. If I had not wanted peace as well, I should not have come here. But the Great White Father must tell his children to keep the peace; if they had not come into our lands there never would have been any trouble between us. You have your land fenced in and you do not want us to come on it. We, too, do not want you to bother us. I want peace. I speak for all my people."

It was then the turn of the man from Washington to speak:

"I have come here because the Great White Father, my President, has sent me to talk with you. It is a long way from his house, but my journey has not been in vain when I find we both share the desire for peace between us. He has told me to tell you that he does not wish to buy any more of your land, but simply to live in peace. I bring you many wagonloads of presents as a mark of his friendship and respect. All that he asks for in return is a trail through your land so that his people may travel to the gold-mining camps in the west. And he also asks that you allow forts to be built beside the trail to guard the peace which we make between us."

Echa! The chiefs were angry. Again the white man had tried to deceive us. First they said they wanted peace, but then they said they wanted a trail leading to the place where they grub like prairie dogs in the earth to find the yellow metal which makes them crazy.

And that was not all. That same day many more soldiers marched into Fort Laramie. Colonel Carrington was their chief. He had come to take the trail which the men from Washington wanted and he had brought along two scouts to lead him into our lands and show the soldiers the best places to build their forts.

Colonel Carrington said he wanted peace, but what do white people mean by peace? How can there be peace when your neighbor demands a way through your land whether you say yes or no? It is not peace when he comes with an arrow fitted to his bow, nor is it peace when you know he will shoot if you do not do as he tells you. Colonel Carrington said he only wanted a strip of land as wide as the wheels of a wagon, and a small place to build the forts. He said it was not much to ask.

It was always so. Years before, in the land to the south which once was ours, they had asked for a way through our lands and we gave it to them. First a few had come. Then more came and a few more had built their houses and had wanted more land to make fences around their spotted buffalo. They told us then that we must keep off the land which was really ours. The prairie was set on fire; the earth plowed up and the trees cut down. More, and always more, had come. A river of white people had swollen into a flood, spreading over the land, killing and driving away the buffalo and the deer, the elk and the antelope, leaving only coyotes to skulk among the rotting carcasses and bleaching bones in a scarred land. And now, again, the white men had come to take away our land; this time to take our best hunting grounds.

They came, marching with guns and long knives, and holding high their flags. They came with saws and axes to cut down the trees, and spades to dig up the earth; they came with white-topped wagons with wheels which squeaked, and with the great wagon guns which speak twice. They came with horse-soldiers and walking-soldiers, singing as they marched, saying in their songs that they would

drive us like buffalo before them and kill us all. With them rode a young soldier-chief, Captain Brown, who laughed much, saying that he would bring back Red Cloud's scalp. And with him rode another chief, Captain Fetterman, who boasted loudly for all to hear that he could whip the whole Sioux Nation with only eighty men. It was brave talk, yet foolish.

We went back to the council the next day and Red Cloud spoke for the last time:

"It must be either peace or war. If you want peace, return at once." Pointing at Colonel Carrington, he said, "The Great White Father sends us presents and wants us to sell him the Trail, but you come with soldiers to steal it before we say yes or no! You must understand that the Sioux, and especially the Oglalas, have many warriors.

"We are brave and ready to fight for our lands. We are not afraid of your men, nor of the young soldier-chief who threatens and makes big boast of killing us all with only eighty men. Many warriors are ready to meet you. Every family will send its young men and they all will say of the Great White Father's dogs, 'Let them come!'

"I will talk with you no more. I will go now and I will fight you. As long as I live, I will fight you for the last hunting grounds of my people."

We left Fort Laramie after that because we knew there was going to be trouble. Sitting Bull and Crazy Horse had been right; we should never have gone to talk with the white men. I was young then and I did not understand all

these things. I remember I was thinking most about the presents and the guns we never had and the white man's food I did not eat. But when I look back now, I know Red Cloud was right not to take the presents; he would not sell our lands for a few pretty things to give to his wife. He was a great chief who always decided what was best for his people.

Red Cloud led us north to the mouth of Prairie Dog Creek. It was the Moon of Ripening Cherries, July, the time when we hold our Sun Dance every year. It is then that the sun begins to go back from its highest place in the sky and the time of year when the sage covering the prairie is fully grown and the buffalo roll their great bodies in its fragrant leaves. Everything in nature rejoices: the birds, the animals, the trees and flowers and also the little things which crawl. We know that the Great Spirit created all these, and, above all, the sun which gives life to all things. In the Sun Dance we join the whole universe in rejoicing and giving thanks.

I think we had all forgotten about the soldiers during those happy days. Yet it was not long afterwards that scouts came into camp bringing news that the soldiers were already building a fort (Fort Philip Kearny) on the Piney Fork of Powder River, about an easy day's ride south of our camp. When Red Cloud heard this he sent out runners to the Miniconjous and to our allies the Cheyennes and Arapahoes, calling them to a council of war.

It was one of the greatest gatherings of the tribes in the memory of the old men. I was not a chief in those days and I did not go to sit outside the council tipi. I heard later that every chief had spoken for war against the soldiers and that they had all smoked the war pipe.

There were many small fights that summer, but no great victory. And yet I shall never forget one fight we had with the soldiers a few days after the great council of war. I had left camp with my cousin Slow Buffalo and some of our friends to see what the soldiers were doing down on Piney Creek. They had already built a fence higher than a man can reach, with sharp points along the top which went around their lines of little white tents. All day long we heard the sound of chopping wood and trees falling in the forests far up the creek where it leaves the Big Horn Mountains. We stayed out among the hills looking down on the soldiers driving their wagons to and fro along the trail like ants, shouting and cracking their long whips as they brought back the trees to build their houses inside the fence. They did not see us through the dust raised by their wagons. Just before dark, when the last wagon had returned to the fort, the horses were driven inside and the gates were closed. In a little while the soldiers went to stand in rows on the bare place in the center, and their flag floated down from the top of the tall pole while a soldier blew notes on a bugle. After that silence fell.

The next morning, we led our horses silently down the creek among the willows. We could not get close to the fort because there was a soldier with a gun across his shoulder looking over the fence. So we tied up our horses and waited, hiding near the place where the soldiers came down to the creek to fetch water. Perhaps a soldier would come and we could capture his gun.

Toke! Listen! We had only been there a little while when we heard the sound of white men shouting. Have they seen us? The gate swings open and a soldier comes out. He is calling to someone inside. Look! Horses are coming out, many horses, and many more horses following them, and, behind the last, four soldiers driving them! So many horses and only four soldiers to guard them. The soldiers are careless. I asked Slow Buffalo in a whisper if it was a dream which I saw, but he said he thought it must be real and that we should try to stampede the herd.

We led our horses across the creek toward them and waited, hiding behind a bank, until they were close, so close that I could hear one of the soldiers yawn. The leading horses had nearly reached the creek and I can see them still; they are tall strong-looking horses. Now! *Hoka Hey!* Fan out and charge! Make lots of noise! Wave your buffalo robe to frighten the horses! They turn, slowly at first, the ones in front getting in the way of those following behind. But it was the sound of the guns cracking in the stillness of the early morning air which set them galloping in a wide half-circle away from the creek. The soldiers did not even have time to reload; two were down at the first charge, one with my arrow sticking through his neck and another lanced by Slow Buffalo. I did not see the others after that and the sound of the bugle coming from inside the fort seemed far behind.

The herd galloped faster and always faster along the trail where the soldiers had been hauling timber the day before, and we followed after in the dust and thunder of hooves, yelling and whipping those behind. I was excited! I think they were the happiest moments of my life and I yelled until my throat was dry.

We drove them hard and it was about the middle of the afternoon when we reached camp. The horses were tired but we set them galloping again as we drove them through the entrance and all the way around the inside of the camp circle. All the people came running from the tipis to see, the women making the tremolo and the young boys shouting and laughing as they jumped on the soldiers' horses and galloped them round and round the camp. The warriors and the old men came forward to look and to examine the iron shoes and to wonder over the marks burnt with hot irons into the horses' flanks. Everyone was happy, and we felt proud when Red Cloud told us it was a good thing we had done. That night the whole camp joined in the victory songs and dancing.

All through the summer we made life hard for them. If the soldiers wanted water from the creek, they had to fight for it. If they wanted timber for their houses from the forests, or grass for their horses from the valley bottom, they gave their blood for it. If they needed food from Fort Laramie, they had to fight their way up the trail. And if they hunted fresh meat, their hunters returned more hunted than hunting. We made them prisoners inside their own fort. Hardly a day passed when our young men looking down from the hills did not see another long wooden box carried from the fort to be buried on the bare slopes outside. Yet it made no difference; there always seemed to be more white men coming from where those first ones came.

Late in the Moon of Falling Leaves, November, when the buffalo hunts were over and the meat packs were filled for the winter, the hunting bands of the Oglalas and the Miniconjous came together again. We tried to draw the soldiers away from the shadow of their fort with the great guns which looked out through holes in the fence. We could not fight against those with bows and arrows, tomahawks and knives. Red Cloud sent out warriors as decoys to draw the soldiers away to a place among the hills where more warriors waited, hiding in ambush. But the soldiers would not follow. The days passed, and our young men became impatient with waiting so long. "Where is the young soldier-chief, Captain Fetterman, who boasts that he can ride through the whole Sioux Nation with only eighty men?" taunted those who knew a little white-man talk, riding in close to the fort under the big guns. "And where is the other one who says he will take Red Cloud's scalp? Why does he not come and take it?"

Then one day the soldiers did follow the decoys led by Crazy Horse. It was the young soldier-chief, Captain Fetterman, who led the soldiers and they followed the decoys almost into our ambush, when some of our young impatient ones started shooting too soon. We chased them back into the fort, but the plan to trap them had failed and the chiefs were angry with the young men.

The winter was moving south and soon it would be too cold to fight the soldiers again that year. The mornings were bright and clear and the Big Horn Mountains, with new snow in the high meadows, seemed only a short ride away to the west. Already the trees stood bare beside creeks and the birds searched hurriedly for little things to eat among the dead leaves soon to be frozen over.

Red Cloud talked with the chiefs. He planned to try once again to draw the soldiers into the hills. But many shook their heads; "Now the soldiers know our plan and they will not follow the decoys a second time." I, too, did not think the young soldier-chief would be so foolish as to walk again into the trap. "Then let us ask the medicine-man who has far-seeing eyes to see what is to be," said Red Cloud. "Let him tell us."

And so the medicine-man was called to the council tipi. I had been frightened of this mysterious person when a boy, because he always dressed in women's clothes, but he was much respected by the tribes for his great powers of making magic and looking into the future. Word spread quickly around the camp that he had ridden out into the hills, looking with inward eyes to foretell whether we would kill any soldiers. People gathered to hear what he would say.

After a little while he rode back to where the chiefs were waiting, sitting on their horses. "I have ten dead soldiers, five in each hand," he said, stretching his arms before him, "Do you want them?" Red Cloud was angry. "Do you not see," he said, "that there are many too many warriors here to share so few soldiers?" and he whipped the medicine-man's horse away, telling him to look for a great victory with many dead soldiers. Three times the medicine-man returned, and each time Red Cloud sent him away to look again. He was gone a long time and I wondered what he would foretell.

Perhaps he was frightened of Red Cloud and did not say what he really saw. And then he came, a fourth time, galloping down from a hill behind us, blowing shrill notes on an eagle-bone whistle. He fell from his horse in front of the chiefs and said, "I have a hundred dead soldiers in my hands," and at that everyone cheered. It was what we had been waiting for, and everyone ran forward, trying to be the first to touch the enemy held in the hollow of his hands. The medicine-man had said it, and he was never wrong. And the fight we were to have with the soldiers the next day is still remembered as the Battle of the Hundred in the Hands.

We left camp early. It was cold, with a wind which had a feeling of snow coming, and the sun shone without warmth between dark cloud ridges. There was ice on the creek, and the sparkling grass and dead leaves crackled under our horses' hooves. White men have often asked how many there were that day fighting the soldiers. I do not know. There were very many. Maybe a man could have gone on counting until he reached almost one thousand.

We stopped where the white man's trail comes down the steep ridge of Ambush Hill into the narrow valley of Peno Creek. It was there that the soldiers had nearly been trapped a few days before. Red Cloud sent warriors ahead to attack the wagons used for hauling timber. When the warriors saw the soldiers coming out of the fort to defend the wagons, they were to retreat and leave the decoys to coax the soldiers into our ambush. It was a difficult and dangerous thing the decoys had to do.

It was very cold. We squatted with our backs turned against the wind which was rushing up the ravines where we were hiding on either side of the trail. The chiefs rode along the hills telling the young men to stay hidden and not to shoot until the signal was given. This time there must be no mistake. Little Horse, the Cheyenne chief who had made a vow not to retreat in the fight, would give the signal. When he stood up and waved his lance above his head, then would be the moment.

I looked up at the sky and the rolling clouds and I knew snow was coming. We sat still as the rocks around us.

A shot! Then more, far off! It was the warriors attacking the wagons. After a while there was silence, and more waiting. Perhaps the soldiers would not follow the decoys after all. An eagle shrieked as he glided with curling wingtips low along the ridge. It was a sign; had he seen the soldiers coming? He flies higher than all other birds and sees everything that moves below him.

When it was seen from the fort that the wood train was under attack, Captain Fetterman was ordered to go and relieve it. His contempt for the Indians' fighting ability was well known and Colonel Carrington had misgivings about sending him. His orders were explicit: "Support the wood train. Relieve it and report to me. Do not engage or pursue Indians at its expense. Under no circumstances pursue over Lodge Trail Ridge." The orders were read out and then repeated before they were handed over in writing.

Instead of advancing directly along the wood road to relieve the wagon train, Captain Fetterman led his force behind Sullivant Hills, with the evident intention of crossing over the hills and attacking the Indians from the rear. When the Indian scouts on Sullivant Hills saw Fetterman's advance, they signaled the warriors attacking the wood train to withdraw. They separated, the main party retreating north, leaving the decoys to entice the soldiers into the ambush. Captain Fetterman had orders not to pursue the Indians, but he now had eighty-two men under his command, sufficient for him to gain the glory he was seeking.

After what seemed a long time there were more shots, always a little closer as the decoys drew the soldiers toward us. I slipped my bow from its case and strung it ready. My horse was restless; he, too, knew there was going to be a fight. I took his head between my hands and spoke to him softly, "We are in danger; obey me in everything. If you have to run for your life and mine, do your best, and if we return I shall give you an eagle feather to tie in your mane." He was quiet after that. All the warriors were making ready, pulling the covers from their shields and tying their buffalo robes around their waists. My cousin, Slow Buffalo, stood next to me, whistling his medicine song through his teeth to strengthen his heart.

There they are! Ten warriors standing against the sky and shooting back at soldiers close behind them. See, it is the young soldier-chief, Captain Fetterman, who holds up his arm for them to stop up there on the ridge. This time he leads eighty soldiers, and more.

The decoys charged up close under the soldiers' guns. Crazy Horse was leading. Another, a Cheyenne, seemed to ride right among the soldiers until I thought he would be hit. A soldier toppled from his saddle, and then the decoys were galloping back again, down toward the trail to make the soldiers follow.

The soldiers advanced, their horses picking their way carefully down the steep slope, with the walking soldiers marching in lines behind. We held our horses' mouths so they would not neigh at the strange horses. Will the young ones hold back a little longer? Everything is still; there is only the creak of saddles and the clink of iron horseshoes against the stones and hard frozen earth. The leading soldiers have reached the trail. Now they are between us. Little Horse, who will give the signal, still has not moved. I pull the arrow tighter against the bowstring. The decoys have turned around and are climbing back again, up the trail toward the soldiers. It is time!

There! Little Horse shakes his lance above his head. I jerk the arrow back and it flies from my bow and then is lost among the hundreds joining it. My second arrow follows quickly before the first has hit, and after it another, and then another joins the cloud of arrows falling like wind-whipped hailstones among and all around the soldiers down there on the trail. The sound of all those arrows comes back even now to my ears; it is a sound like no other sound I have ever heard and it is bad to remember. It is mixed up with many guns going off and people shouting, the sound of horses and men in agony, and above it all the sharp notes of the bugle many times repeated.

I think the soldiers were too surprised and frightened to shoot back. For a long moment they stood, not knowing what to do. They did not have a chance. Many died right there before they had fired their first shot. If our arrows missed one soldier, then the other next to him would fall because they were bunched up together in lines where they had stopped. I remember seeing a horse with arrows sticking in him and crazy with pain break from the lines and charge off down the trail straight into the decoys. The soldier tried desperately to rein him back, but fell from the saddle full of arrows; his horse dragged him bumping over the frozen earth. It was bad.

And then all the soldiers turned and were running, running back up the trail toward the fort, the horse-soldiers leaving the walking-soldiers behind. Everything happened fast. I joined the warriors rushing down on both sides toward the blue lines of soldiers on the trail. Suddenly those near me were shouting to stop and everyone was jerking back on the reins and bumping into those in front; arrows, shot by our friends on the other side of the trail, were whistling among us. Ghost Wolf, out in front, had fallen with an arrow sticking through his neck. Another man, whose name I do not remember, had his horse killed under him with an arrow which went through a soft place in his leg. We rode back quickly, out of the way, and skirted behind the soldiers.

The horse-soldiers left the trail and climbed up the side where the Cheyennes had been hiding. They kept close together; our arrows could not miss them. Soldiers always fight that way; they do not zig-zag their horses to avoid being hit. It is a strange way to fight and stay alive. But they fought bravely. Many fell on the way and those who reached the jutting rocks of the ridge were surrounded by the Cheyennes. It was the same with the walking-soldiers. They scrambled after the horse-soldiers, turning and dropping onto one knee to shoot back. They fought hard all the way; the dead and wounded littered their tracks up the ravine. They never did catch up with the horse-soldiers; they turned to fight where there are some large rocks standing in a circle.

I remember well how one brave soldier, with long hair on his face, gave his life so that the others could have time to climb higher up the ridge. The story has been told many times. He had a many-shot pistol in each hand and was pointing them first at one of us, and then at another, and jumping from side to side and shouting with the biggest voice I have ever heard. He fought more like an Indian than a white man and it seemed that our arrows could not touch him. It was that soldier who killed Fearless Bear and Red Eagle. When he had no more bullets left, Charging Eagle, an Oglala chief, rode up and shot an arrow into him. But the soldier did not fall. He was hard to kill. He broke off the arrow where it was sticking in his shoulder and, running forward, he pulled Charging Eagle out of his saddle and killed him

with many blows from the butt of his empty pistol. It was a brave thing to do, but he died after that with many arrows sticking in him.

The sky was like night coming, with snow driving hard across the valley. The walking-soldiers were well hidden among the gray rocks and the little piles of driven snow. Above where they were hiding, their flag flapped like something alive in the wind, a bit of bright color against the dark earth. I could just see their white faces as they took aim over the rocks, and the puffs of gunsmoke and frozen breath whipped away up the valley with the slanting snow. It was very cold, so cold that the gun barrels turned white with frost.

Red Cloud was out in front shouting, "Let's get it done; only the rocks live forever," and we charged right up to the circle of rocks, shooting in among the soldiers. But their guns were too many for us and we had to go back. Several riders were already down. When we charged up again, I noticed that my horse did not seem to feel my whip and suddenly he fell, the blood freezing as it flowed from a hole in his side made by a soldier's bullet. He was a good horse. It made me sad. Bullets were flying all about me and I got down out of the way behind his warm body. I pulled the eagle feather from my hair and tied it to his mane.

After that every warrior left his horse to crawl up to the soldiers and surround them. I was so cold that I could not feel my fingers against the bowstring. Then High Backbone, war-chief of the Miniconjous, got up and started running, shouting for us to follow. "Now is a good time to die!" *Hoka Hey!* We were all running up among the rocks and jumping from side to side to dodge soldiers' bullets. I was just behind the leading ones and for a moment I could not see the soldiers, but then the few who were left alive were up and we were fighting them hand to hand. High Backbone was first among them. He struck like lightning to left and right around him and I saw a soldier fall beneath his heavy stone-headed tomahawk.

A soldier rose up right in front of me. I did not have time to shoot. He raised his empty gun above his head and I jumped aside as it shattered on the rocks where I had been. He shouted something in white-man talk which I did not understand. He was picking up a stone to throw at me when I knocked him forward with my bow. I jumped on top of him and he panted like a buffalo bull as I drove my knife into him; once, twice, three times and he went limp.

There were only a few more shots up under the ridge where the Cheyennes were fighting the last of the horse-soldiers. My arrows were all gone and I did not join them. Then suddenly there was shouting, and a soldier who was not dead was up again and fighting with Swift Hawk. The soldier had lost his gun and had only a bugle for a club. I do not think Swift Hawk felt brave when he stabbed him with his knife. We saw that he was an old man who should have stayed back beside his fire while his grandchildren fought. He had died bravely, and a warrior covered his body with a buffalo robe.

It was all over. But a dog nobody had noticed before and which had come with the soldiers ran whimpering up the trail toward the fort. He ran, looking back for those who would never follow him again. "Let him tell the other dogs at the fort what has happened here," said Red Cloud. But nothing was to return that day, and he fell with an arrow through his body, a small and silent thing among the rocks and snow.

Everyone picked up the guns which were lying around. I found one, and we searched for ammunition among the dead soldiers. I pulled off a soldier's blue coat with brass buttons. Inside the pocket there was a knife which folded up. It was pretty, with a handle made of shell and a long chain hanging from one end. In another pocket I found a leather pouch with a little picture of a white woman holding a baby and five young children standing close. They looked happy. I left the picture beside the soldier, but the memory of it does not leave me.

We looked at the dead soldiers and at their two young chiefs lying close together. They looked very young to lead so many men; we too have had young chiefs who were foolish in their bravery.

It was a great victory. It had been just as the medicine-man had foretold.

Standing on that peaceful and beautiful hill today there is a monument which the white people have built to remember their dead soldiers. Men and women and little children climb from the road to read the writing on the metal shield and to be photographed beside the monument. They stand, smiling and unthinking, on the earth and the growing grass which remembers the warm blood of those brave soldiers spilled there that day.

I have sent my heart back over the years; the fight has come back as from the dead, but now it has been retold, it will go back to the dead to remain forever.

There is no more to say.

Red Cloud's War is the only instance in the history of the United States where the government has gone to war and afterwards negotiated a peace conceding everything demanded by the enemy and exacting nothing in return.

Doane Robinson

CONCLUSION

Throughout the summer of 1867 the siege continued, and no white men dared to use the Bozeman Trail. A similar state of siege existed at the other forts along the trail. The army, trained to fight conventional pitched battles, had not learned to fight an enemy who employs hit-and-run tactics. The soldiers left the forts only when it was necessary to cut grass or timber. It was on such an occasion, on the 2nd of August, 1867, that Captain Powell and twenty-eight soldiers guarding the woodcutters, were attacked by an overwhelming force of Red Cloud's warriors. The soldiers had just been issued with new breech-loading rifles, and it was these "medicine guns," as the Indians called them, which enabled the soldiers to defend themselves successfully. The Wagon Box Fight was a defeat for the Indians, but it confirmed Washington's fears that Red Cloud was determined to continue the siege.

The army was still smarting from its defeat in the Fetterman Fight and further humiliated by the inability of its forces to defend the Bozeman Trail. The generals were eager to launch a massive campaign against the Sioux, but Washington realized that such an offensive would be costly and long-drawn-out and they were not prepared to sanction it. Instead, they ordered the forts to be abandoned. By the Treaty of 1868 the Bozeman Trail was closed and the Powder River country given back to the Indians. It was a triumph for Red Cloud.

The land for which he had fought so hard was solemnly promised to his people forever. He had succeeded in holding back the white people—for a time, but he knew his people could never win the final struggle soon to come.

Washington soon forgot the treaty and the soldiers marched again, but Red Cloud never went back on the promise he had given to fight no more.

Paul Goble has written and illustrated the following books:

Red Hawk's Account of Custer's Last Battle	1969
Brave Eagle's Account of the Fetterman Fight	1972
Lone Bull's Horse Raid	1973
The Friendly Wolf	1974
The Girl Who Loved Wild Horses	1978
The Gift of the Sacred Dog	1980
Star Boy	1983
Buffalo Woman	1984
The Great Race of the Birds & Animals	1985
Death of the Iron Horse	1987
Her Seven Brothers	1988
Iktomi and the Boulder	1988
Beyond the Ridge	1989
Iktomi and the Berries	1989
Dream Wolf	1990
Iktomi and the Ducks	1990
Iktomi and the Buffalo Skull	1991
I Sing for the Animals	1991
Crow Chief	1992

DUE DA

Printed in USA